Military-school uniform.

Traditional white communion attire.

Karol Józef Wojtyla as a boy.

Plate 1

Everyday school wear.

Altar boy's robe.

Plate 2

As a student at the Wadowice Gymnasium.

(This costume fits over the doll at the right.)

As a student at the Jagiellonian University.

Plate 3

Dressed for work in a stone quarry.

Plate 4

Costume for a production of the play *Knight of the Moon*.

Ordination robes.

The black collar is covered by an amice (oblong white linen vestment), worn under the alb (full-length white linen vestment). A deacon's stole is worn over one shoulder and held in place by a knotted and tasseled cincture (belt or rope worn about the waist). Upon ordination, the deacon's stole is moved to the other side.

Theology student's cassock.

Plate 5

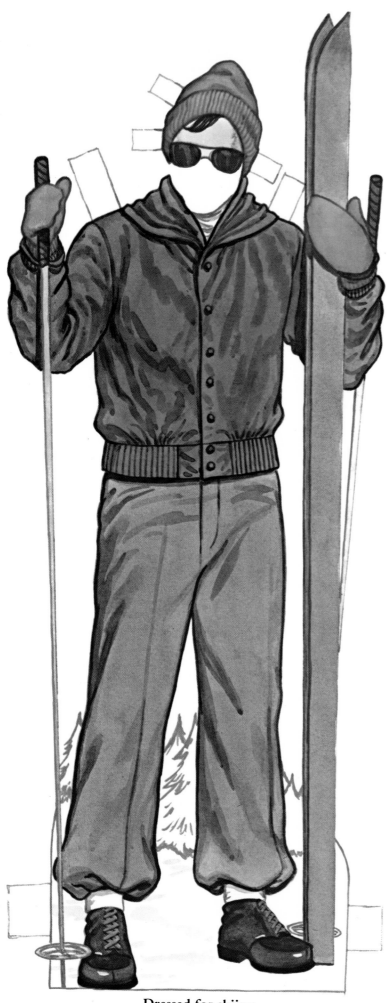

Dressed for skiing.

(This costume fits over the doll at the right.)

Plate 6

A "house" cassock.

Father Wojtyla upon being named Auxiliary Bishop of Krakow.

Archiepiscopal attire.
Archbishop Wojtyla dressed for his visit to Chicago.

Basic cardinal's attire.
The hat is called a biretta.

Plate 7

Cardinal's attire.

Cardinal Wojtyla is wearing a simar (a special kind of cassock with a short cape) and a rochet (a close-fitting white linen garment ornamented with lace).

Plate 8

Cardinal's attire.

Upon the election of Pope John Paul I.

Pontifical attire

As Pope John Paul II. The pope's simar, always white, is worn with a broad, ornamental cincture. The skullcap is properly called a calotte or zucchetto.

Plate 9

Pontifical attire.

John Paul's first appearance to the public as pope. His attire was composed of a white cassock, a red mozzetta (a short cape, buttoned over the breast, with a small hood attached) and a stole of red satin with metallic embroidery.

Plate 10

Pontifical attire.

Wearing the pontifical hat of red velvet trimmed with gold and a
gold-trimmed cloak and cape, specially for winter use. The pope's
hand covers a pectoral cross.

Plate 11

Pontifical attire.

John Paul II wore this embroidered stole on his visit to Ireland.

Plate 12

Pontifical attire.

This stole, elaborately embroidered with iconographic designs,
was specially created for his visit to Poland.

Plate 13

Pontifical attire.

The green chasuble was worn for Ordinary Mass in Washington, D.C. The headdress is called a miter. Around the neck and over the chasuble is a special band called a pallium.

Plate 14

Pontifical attire.

Wearing the gold chasuble for High Mass.

Plate 15

Hats worn on various occasions.

The rather battered hat (top left) was often worn by Bishop Wojtyla on his travels. The giant sombrero (top right) and elaborate Indian headdress (bottom) were donned by John Paul during his official Mexican visit.

Plate 16